Bygone PARTICK 2

by

BILL SPALDING

The first record of a Partick bridge over the Kelvin dates from 1577. This bridge was eventually demolished, in 1895, during the construction of the Lanarkshire and Dumbartonshire lines of the Caledonian Railway. By 1797 the old bridge was no longer suitable for 'modern traffic' and a new one was built further north. It can be seen here on the left and still stands today. The more substantial bridge on the right was built, alongside the previous bridge, to cope with the ever-increasing traffic of the developing burgh. It is the present road bridge. On the parapets there are four commemorative plaques, two at each end, facing the road. They give some details about the bridge's construction, including the fact that it was erected by the Trustees of the Partick and Yoker Turnpike Roads.

© 1992 Bill Spalding
First Published in the United Kingdom, 1992
Reprinted 1995
By Richard Stenlake, Ochiltree Sawmill, The Lade, Ochiltree, Ayrshire KA18 2NX
Tel: 01290 700266

ISBN 1-872074-21-9

Partick Bridge and Art Galleries.

This picture shows that the bridge originally had a lamp on top of the central plinth on each side. The picture probably dates from around 1901, because the Art Galleries are present and although there are tramlines, there are not yet any overhead wires for electric trams.

INTRODUCTION

Partick became established as a village because of two things. Firstly, the River Kelvin, the main obstacle on the ancient road between Glasgow and Dumbarton, was easily crossed at this point and secondly, the establishment of the mills on the river.

In the mid-1880s it grew into a small town due to the establishment of the shipyards. It is rather ironic that although the shipyards have all disappeared, at the foot of Partick Bridge Street, one flour mill still remains.

Featured in this volume are several postcards of Victoria (or Whiteinch) Park. Although frequented by Partickonians, Kelvingrove Park was not a Partick park, as is seen from its alternative name, the West End Park. It is in the east end of Partick, but is in the west end of Glasgow, which established the park around the mid-1800s. Victoria Park was opened on the 2nd of July 1887. The day was observed as a public holiday in Partick and a large procession, headed by the Provost and Commissioners, made its way there from the Burgh Hall. The Provost, Andrew McLean, was granted a knighthood.

By the 1920s Glasgow had annexed so many of the surrounding burghs that there was a considerable amount of duplication in street names; at one time there were no fewer than nine Hill Streets. By 1932 the duplication had been more or less eradicated by re-naming some of the streets. Some examples will be mentioned in the following pages.

In this later photograph the second Kelvin Hall, built in 1927, can be seen; the lamps are missing from the bridge, there are overhead wires for electric trams and the style of the women's clothes has changed. As the familiar noticeboard of the Kelvin Hall is not present (it would be behind the lamp-post) this picture may have been taken fairly soon after the hall was opened.

This was built as a western extension of the old Anderson College of Glasgow, which had been founded by Professor John Anderson ('Jolly Jack Phosphorous'). All of the departments of the college were in the city centre's George Street until 1886 when it became the Glasgow and West of Scotland Technical College ('The Tec'). By 1963 it had become the University of Strathclyde. The Partick extension is now under the control of Glasgow University for teaching medical subjects. The tenement on the left, at the corner of Church Street, has been demolished and replaced with an extension of the University, while the ground on the right, behind the railings, is now covered by an extension of the Western Infirmary.

Byres Road

This pre-1910 photograph shows the shops at the corners of Havelock Street. Outside one of them is what seems like a kind of wheelbarrow with a large milk can; it was possibly used for deliveries. Several of the shops on the right are now restaurants.

It can just be made out that this view of Lawrence Street is at the corner of Alexandra (Elie) Street. The white lettering fixed to the windows of the dairy is of interest. On the Elie Street window it says: 'NATIONAL TELEPHONE/ CALL HERE/LOCAL CALLS 1d EACH'. The righthand window says: 'UNDER MEDICAL SUPERVISION'. The centre window has the rather cryptic (to me): 'WARM MILK/EVERY AFTERNOON/AT 4.30'. The railings in the gardens on both sides of the street were removed 'for the war effort' during World War II.

Highburgh Road

This view of Highburgh Road looks westwards from Byres Road, with which it used to form a T-junction. Traffic can now cross Byres Road directly into University Avenue. When the junction was re-designed, the tenement facing Highburgh Road and the buildings on the south side of Ashton Road were removed. The Western Telephone Exchange was erected in 1907 in the space on the right-hand side of the road.

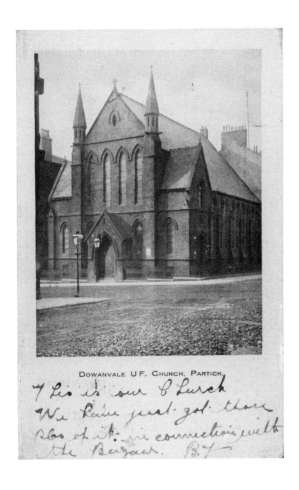

DOWANVALE U.F. CHURCH, PARTICK.

[handwritten note]

This church was erected in 1880. The building is in use today as Partick Highland Free Church. The Rev. James Wallace was a prominent personality in Partick as he was also head-master of the Mission School (also known as the Penny-a-Week School) which was established in Kelvin Street to provide education for the poorer children of the burgh.

REV. JAMES WALLACE,
DOWANVALE U.F. CHURCH, PARTICK.

Hyndland Street, Partick.

In the days of the village this was called The Coarse Loan (Lane). It was re-named because it led to the lands of Hyndland. This view looks northwards from Dumbarton Road and in the distance can be seen the tall steeple of Dowanhill Church; the part of Hyndland Street beyond this used to be called Temple Street. The old name of this part of Dumbarton Road, Crown Place, can be seen above the corner of William McColl's shop. This building has since been demolished. The Quarter Gill public house now stands on the opposite corner.

Hyndland Street, Partick.

White Street is on the right and St. Peter's R.C. Church is on the left.

Looking west can be seen the part of the street, from Hyndland Street to the cul-de-sac, which was called White Street after a Provost of Partick. From Hyndland Street to Dowanhill Street used to be Beaconsfield Street and Dowanvale Terrace. The section between Dowanhill Street and Byres Road was Wood Street. Later the whole street, from Byres Road to the rear of Hamilton Crescent School, was named White Street.

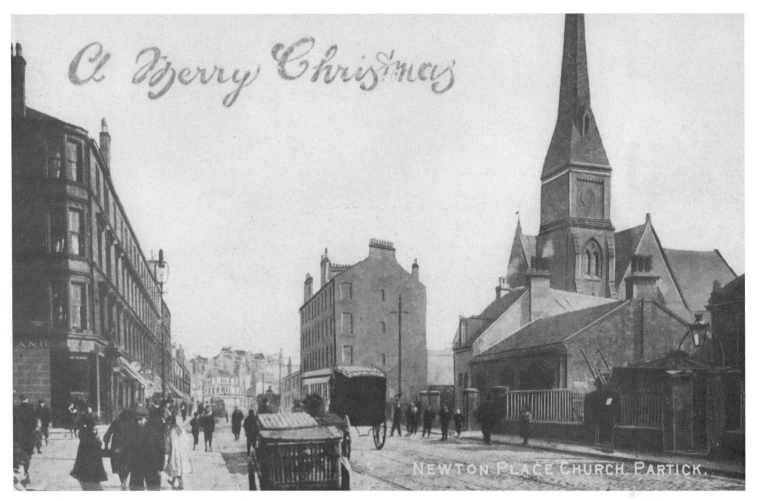

This building was erected on the site of the second church building to be put up in Partick, the Relief Church. It has since been replaced by a smaller building, Partick South Church, which was built in 1988. The first church faced onto Castlebank Street, which was at that time the main road through the village. By the time the second church had been built Dumbarton Road had become the main road.

Gardner Street, Partick.

This street was named after a prominent butcher who was also a commissioner. He bought the mansion house of Muir Park, which was situated at about the level of White Street. The extreme steepness of the hill was used in the 1920s to test buses.

Hamilton Crescent Partick

The lower part of this street was Hamilton Street (later re-named Fortrose Street). The upper part is Hamilton Crescent which contains the West of Scotland Cricket Ground, the Partick Bowling Club and Hamilton Crescent School.

Hamilton Crescent Academy. Partick, Glasgow.

The school was opened in May 1887 and held 1,000 pupils. In April 1912 the staff and pupils were moved to the new school in Hyndland, now Hyndland Secondary. The building in the picture now houses Hyndland Primary School.

Burgh Hall, Partick. RELIABLE SERIES.

In 1869 several sites were considered for the Burgh Halls and Maxwell Street was chosen in preference to Hyndland Street. The building was opened in 1872. In 1902 the tenements in Maxwell Street were converted into public offices and the Lesser Burgh Hall (the 'Wee Burgh') was opened in 1913. The burgh's coat-of-arms reflects some of its history by incorporating a ship, a bishop's mitre, a castle and a wheatsheaf with millstones. Maxwell Street was renamed Burgh Hall Street.

INDUSTRIA DITAT.

ARMORIAL BEARINGS
of the
BURGH OF PARTICK.

Dumbarton Road   Partick

This circa 1904 view looks east along Dumbarton Road from about the top of Merkland Street. To the right is the newsagent's which was also Taylor's West End Library. Up until at least 1960, several newsagents and larger branches of Boot's the Chemist, operated lending libraries. Montgomerie's the bakers, next door, advertises Bermaline Bread in its window. John Montgomerie's Bermaline Bakery was in nearby Vine Street. It was demolished in 1912 and later that year the first Partick Picture House was opened on the site.

U.F. Church, Partick

The congregation started open-air meetings around 1859. They later used the station waiting room, a wooden shed and then a wooden church. Situated behind the cricket ground, this building was opened in March 1869. In 1936 it amalgamated with Partick Dowanvale to form Partick High and Dowanvale. Later it was part of Hamilton Crescent Church and is now joined with Partick South. The building is no longer standing.

Gardner Street, Partick

On the left, at the north-west corner of Muirpark Street, is Gardner Street Church. In 1875 a mission was formed for the Gaelic speaking residents of Partick. After using a corrugated iron church for some time, this building was put up in 1905 as Partick Gaelic U.F. Church. Between 1881 and 1891 the number of Gaelic speakers in Partick rose from 494 to 1,208.

DUMBARTON RD. FROM N.B. RAILWAY BRIDGE.

In the bottom left-hand corner are the tram lines leading from the Partick Tram Depot in Hayburn Street into Dumbarton Road. The shop on the corner was later taken over by D.M. Hoey, the nearby gent's outfitters. On the opposite side of Dumbarton Road are the Thomlinson shops. William Thomlinson had the Greenbank Leather Works (now closed). His brother John had a stationer's business with the Stanley Works behind it in Norval Street. The works still operates today as a box-making firm.

This 1960 picture shows Hayburn Street with the Partick Tram Depot. It was used first by the horse-drawn trams and then by the electric trams. When these stopped running it became Partick Bus Depot. It is now a depot for Regional Council vehicles.

This photograph, also from 1960, features the bridge carrying the railway lines (originally of the North British Railway Company) northwards through Partick Station. This was later re-named Partick Hill Station. Later still the entrance was moved to the foot of Merkland Street to link up with the subway as part of the Strathclyde System. The nearby Rosevale Cinema, advertised on the bridge, was later a bingo hall for a spell and is now a snooker club.

WESTLAND DRIVE. WHITEINCH.

This view looks east along Dumbarton Road from the Whiteinch Tram Terminus at the foot of Westland Drive. On the left are the Shaftesbury Cottages, the western end of the Gordon Park development. This was a series of cottages built by Gordon Oswald, in 1885, for the workers on his Scotstoun Estate. Still in use, these rows of cottages, with their front and back gardens, were in marked contrast to the tenement blocks erected south of Dumbarton Road for the workers of Barclay Curle's shipyard.

RECREATION GROUNDS, POLICE DRILL HALL
& GYMNASIUM, HOZIER ST, PARTICK   Nº 488

This view has been swept away by the formation of the Clydeside Expressway, which leads from the Clyde tunnel to the city. The site is now occupied by Partick Interchange. The children's swings are in Meadowside Public park which was opened in 1896. Hozier Street (Beith Street) was named after William Hozier, who owned a lot of land in this part of Partick.

Dumbarton Road, (from Rosevale Street-looking West) Partick.

This shows Partick West around the time of World War I. Archibald Hoy, Wine Merchant and Italian Warehouseman, was established here in 1840, 12 years before the formation of the burgh. This corner was called Downie Place because it was built by Wylie and Lochhead who married sisters by the name of Downie. The first building on the left side of the picture has been demolished so that traffic can now travel from Crow Road, straight across Dumbarton Road, into Rosevale Street. Modern flats have been built between Rosevale Street and Sandy Road.

Crow Road, Partick.

This picture was taken from Dumbarton Road looking north. Beyond the tenement on the right, is the site associated with the goods and mineral station. The space between the two tenements on the left is now occupied by two churches, Partick Free Church of Scotland and Partick Baptist Church. There appears to be a cab rank on the left-hand side of the road.

Dumbarton Road, (from Crawford Street - looking East) Partick.

This part of Dumbarton Road looks much the same today as it did in this pre-1916 photograph.

DUMBARTON ROAD.
Partick, from Apsley St., looking West.

The low building to the left has been replaced with modern flats and the bridges in the distance have been demolished.

This postcard, sent in 1918, has been wrongly captioned. It should be Apsley Street, named after Apsley House which stood here at one time.

Kennedy. Drive Partick 108

Now Kennoway Drive, this street was named after the prominent Kennedy family. Hugh Kennedy was the 8th provost of the burgh and John Kennedy the 12th. Hugh Kennedy and Sons were public works contractors who built the railway stations and piers at Craigendoran, Gourock and Wemyss Bay.

This building now serves as an annexe of Anniesland College.

Balshagray Avenue, Whiteinch.

This avenue was totally transformed when it was converted into an approach road for the Clyde Tunnel. On the left, just north of George Street, is Victoria Park Church. Both church and street have now disappeared.

War Memorial, Whiteinch

Left: Erected in 1922, the War Memorial has a figure of Victory standing on top of the granite cenotaph.

Right: The Partick Society of Methodists were formed in 1869. Their present church, in Dumbarton Road opposite Crawford Street, was opened in 1882.

St. Brides Parish Church was built in Rosevale Street in the late 1800s as part of the last church expansion scheme for the Parish of Govan. Up until 1834, Partick members of the Established Church had to cross the Clyde to attend their Parish Church, which was at Govan Cross. In that year an Established Church building was erected in Church Street but by the end of the century Partick had expanded so far westwards that St. Bride's was built. It was dedicated in 1897 and in 1902 St. Bride's became a separate Parish. The congregation was dissolved in 1975.

Sent in 1904, this postcard depicting 'winchers' has the comment 'Yum! Yum!' on the reverse. I have never seen a close like this one with two flights of stairs.

OUR CLOSE 10 P.M.

1 PARTICK HILL

Partick Hill.

This picture looks north from the top of Peel Street. Annfield (Banavie) Road is on the right and Hayburn Crescent is to the left. Many of the wealthy businessmen of Partick lived in villas in Partickhill. These included shipyard owners such as David Tod (after whom nearby Tod's Brae was unofficially named) John Henderson and Alexander Stephen.

HAYBURN CRESCENT, PARTICKHILL.

This view looks south and shows the left side of the crescent still undeveloped. In the days of the village the Hay or Hays Burn ran south from Dawsholm, through Broomhill Cross, down the crescent and then down Hayburn Street into the Clyde. Like the other burns of the village, the Hay Burn still runs beneath the houses, having been incorporated into the burgh's sewage system. The vacant space on the left is now Hayburn Park.

Partickhill Bowling Club, which was opened in April 1905, is on the right, the Tennis Club is to the rear. The top of Gardner Street can be seen on the left.

Willowbank Bowling Green, Glasgow, W.

F. W. FYFE, PARTICKHILL

Willow Bank Bowling Club settled here in Dowanside Road, Dowanhill, in 1897. It had previously occupied several different sites around Glasgow.

Entrance to Whiteinch Park.

When Victoria Park was opened in 1877, the ladies of Partick, at a cost of £200, provided these ornamental gates for the entrance in Balshagray Avenue. With the construction of the approach road to the Clyde Tunnel they had to be removed. They were re-erected on the north side of the park facing Airthrey Avenue.

B.630.

VICTORIA PARK, GLASGOW

In 1889 this small pond was provided with two islets to protect the waterfowl and in 1891 it was stocked with trout. The much larger artificial lake was popular with model yacht enthusiasts.

Bandstand, Whiteinch Park.

This combined bandstand, bowl house and shelter was opened in 1908. A brick bow was added in 1930.

The Fossil Grove, Whiteinch.

Glasgow.

These fossil tree stumps and roots were discovered in 1887 as workmen were cutting a road through the strata of sandstone and shale lying along the bottom of a quarry. They are estimated to be about 300 million years old and do not resemble any trees still in existence. A Middle Bronze Age cist cemetery was discovered above the fossil trees. This building with a glass roof was erected to protect the grove on 1 January 1890. Similar stumps have been found elsewhere in the Partick area.

General view of the Rockery, Victoria Park, Glasgow

The Rockery is adjacent to the Fossil Grove. This picture shows how it looked in the early 1900s.

Dumbarton Road from Whiteinch Cross looking West.

Most of this view vanished with the re-development of Whiteinch when the Clyde tunnel was built. These tenements were built mainly to house the workers of Barclay Curle's Clydeholm Shipyard.

Park Drive, N. Whiteinch.

This is now Victoria Park Drive North. In the title the 'N.' refers to Park Drive, not Whiteinch.

VICTORIA PARK GARDENS, NORTH, BROOMHILL, GLASGOW   B 627

Again, there should be no comma between Gardens and North.

Dumbarton Road, Partick West.

This photograph is taken from the foot of Broomhill Drive and shows the end of Thornwood Drive which is now closed to traffic from Dumbarton Road. To the right is the beginning of Sawmill Road, which in the old days led to Partick Sawmills. At one time it was called the Ree Road. Granny Gibb's Cottage was situated about here in the days of the village. It was an overnight stop for the West Highland drovers on their way to the cattle market in Glasgow. There has been a lot of demolition and re-development here in connection with an approach way to the Clyde tunnel.

47

Broomhill Avenue, Partick West

On the right are the janitor's house and swimming pool building of Balshagray School. The building in the distance is on Broomhill Drive, which had previously been called Oswaldhill Road. It has been demolished and high flats now occupy the site. These were built to accommodate some of those whose homes were demolished during the construction of the Clyde Tunnel.

Woodcroft Avenue, Broomhill, Glasgow

The avenue is called after Woodcroft House which used to stand here. The message on this postcard refers to 'nice green fields' opposite the houses. They have since provided the sites for Broomhill Primary School and its annexe, with a row of terraced houses in between.

St. Peter's R. C. School, Partick

Opened in 1899 behind the church in Hyndland Street, this school catered for girls and infants. The nuns from Notre Dame Convent, in nearby Dowanhill, were in charge. Boys attended the school in Partick Bridge Street.

Stewartville Public School   Partick

This was opened in 1893 as a non-denominational school. It became St. Peter's School for boys in 1924 when the Bridge Street school was no longer suitable. It was closed in 1981 and by 1986 had been converted into 46 flats.

This ship, the T.S.S. Transylvania, belonged to the Anchor Line. It was founded in 1838 by Nicol and Robert Handyside and later joined by Thomas Henderson. The Anchor Line house flag made its first appearance in 1856. It had three links in a chain to represent the three partners. When John Henderson became a partner the links were increased to four. In 1872 they bought the Meadowside shipyard of Tod and McGregor where they built hulls. The engines were constructed in Finnieston. In 1916 they joined up with the Donaldson Line, which covered the route to Canada.